GLASGOW
City Beautiful

John McDermott has been taking photographs of Glasgow for over 15 years and has a well-established company, **www.YouKeepEveryPhoto.com**.

In addition, John is a writer and a composer, with such contributions as *Seb*, a novel about a Glasgow boy currently being considered as a screen play by the BBC, and a new rock opera *Jesus Christ Risen Star*, hopefully to be staged at the Edinburgh Festival next year (2008).

He is a double graduate from the University of Glasgow with two degrees, Bachelor of Science Honours in Biochemistry and Bachelor of Divinity with distinction, followed by two years' research in Theology.

John is at his happiest when he is holding a camera, directing his subjects to participate in his works of art.

His other sites include
* www.iLoveGlasgow.com
* www.GlasgowCityBeautiful.com
* www.KiltedPhotographer.com
* www.JohnMcDermott.co.uk

D1225507

GLASGOW
City Beautiful

John McDermott

breedon **books**
PUBLISHING

First published in Great Britain in 2007 by The Breedon Books Publishing
Company Limited Breedon House, 3 The Parker Centre, Derby, DE21 4SZ.

To my mum.
Thank you for all your help over the years.

ISBN 978-1-85983-598-2
Printed and bound by Cromwell Press Ltd, Trowbridge, Wiltshire.

Contents

Foreword

GLASGOW
CHAMBER OF COMMERCE

Glasgow City Beautiful is the definitive insider's handbook to one of Britain's most beautiful cities. The full-colour sections introduce many of Glasgow's highlights with expert coverage of all the sights, from the city centre to George Square, Glasgow Green to the Glasgow Cathedral, the University of Glasgow to the Kelvingrove Museum and Art Galleries to the attractions of its main parks throughout the city.

There are few books that cover Glasgow in such detail and with such spectacular photographs as *Glasgow City Beautiful*. When I realised that every photograph had been taken during the month of February 2007, I knew that Glasgow would be portrayed as fresh, up-to-date and the book would be accurate. It covers such subjects as:

• Architecture and famous architects such as Charles Rennie Mackintosh and Alexander 'Greek' Thomson.

• Landmarks for example the spires of Glasgow Cathedral and the University of Glasgow.

• Places of interest for tourists and locals.

• Parks with such features as the 300 million-year-old fossil grove.

• Museums ranging from the world-famous Kelvingrove Museum and Art Galleries and the Burrell Collection.

• Glasgow's rivers – the Clyde and the Kelvin.

The book is unreservedly accessible and has a good narrative with some unique commentary, and the photographs are the highlight. Tourists and Glaswegians alike will be attracted to this book, with each page being turned with delight and joy. Having been inspired by this book, I am motivated to look up and around at the amazing sights I used to take for granted.

I am delighted that Glasgow has been portrayed in this book as a vibrant and flourishing city. Glasgow is indeed a 'City Beautiful'.

Norman Quiry

President Glasgow Chamber of Commerce

Introduction

Glasgow flourishes indeed. It is one of the most beautiful cities in the world, and I count myself lucky to be a Glaswegian. I have taken over 20,000 photographs of Glasgow over two decades. However, all the photographs in this book were taken during the month of February 2007. While taking the photographs I realised that I knew only a small piece of Glasgow. There are so many parks, statues, inscriptions, stories, many buildings dating from as far back as the 15th century, and, of course, the 300-million-year-old fossilised trees in Victoria Park, in the west end of the city.

The book looks at several elements of Glasgow's history, lifestyle and architecture. Firstly, it has a brief look at Glasgow's history, including how the Romans colonised Glasgow during the period AD142–165. It covers life in and around Glasgow Green then takes the reader through the Glasgow University building, its cloisters and sculptures, and it captures the landmark tower from many viewpoints throughout the city.

The city boasts many famous architects, including Charles Rennie Mackintosh and Alexander (Greek) Thomson, and the book looks at their most important works and that of other famous architects.

You will then be taken along Glasgow's famous streets in the city centre and the West End, including the famous Sauchiehall Street, Buchanan Street and Byres Road. Then on to the centre of Glasgow, George Square, with its many statues and the Glasgow City Chambers. The book also explores parts of Glasgow which are relatively unknown, including Garnethill and the Italian Centre.

Glasgow boasts many museums, including the Burrell collection, St Mungo's Museum of Religious Life and Art, People's Palace and the Kelvingrove Art Gallery, and these are covered in great detail. The book also examines residential areas of Glasgow, in particular tenements, shops, leafy side streets and an overflow development in the north of the city, Drumchapel. It also visits the many parks of Glasgow: the famous Botanic Gardens and the Kibble Palace, Kelvingrove Park and its many fountains and statues, and Victoria Park with the aforementioned Fossil Grove.

Finally, the book covers the two main rivers, the famous Clyde and the Kelvin, and the Forth and Clyde Canal.

After looking at these photographs I encourage you to visit the places for yourself. If you are a tourist or a native, stop, look and admire, and you too will have to admit that Glasgow flourishes, indeed.

Glasgow's History

Glasgow has a rich history, from the time of the fossilised trees in 300 million BC, to the Romans in the second century AD and to the building of Glasgow Cathedral and Provand's Lordship in 1197.

Glasgow Cathedral

Victoria Park

Glasgow's history can be traced back to when Victoria Park was being built. It was then that some fossilised trees were discovered, which are over 300 million years old. The trees grew in a climate similar to the Everglades of Florida, as at the time the equator was close to Glasgow. Victoria Park was built around these fossilised trees, and since then other trees were planted at the turn of the century, which are therefore not quite as old as the fossilised ones yet.

Victoria Park was opened in 1887 to commemorate the Jubilee of Queen Victoria.

There are many beautiful flowerbeds and paths located within Victoria Park. The Clyde Tunnel under the River Clyde was built to replace the Rotundas and took away a large section of the east end of the park.

The Fossil Grove

The Fossil Grove is located among some beautiful scenery. There is another entrance around the back beside a small pond. The Fossil Grove is open during the summer months only.

A building to house the fossilised trees was opened on 1 January 1890. Pictured here is the main entrance to the fossil grove.

The Antonine Wall

Moving forward a few million years, the Romans occupied Glasgow in the second century AD. Exposed footings of the Antonine Wall can still be seen at Hillfoot in Bearsden.

It is clear to see exactly how big the wall was and how much detail went into building it. It was while expanding the cemetery on Boclair Road in 1903 that these portions of the ancient wall were found. Further to the west there is evidence of the wall heading away from the cemetery.

ANTONINE WALL

THE ANTONINE WALL WAS BUILT IN THE 140s AD BY THE ROMAN ARMY ON THE ORDERS OF THE EMPEROR ANTONINUS PIUS. IT RAN FOR 60 km FROM BO'NESS ON THE FORTH TO OLD KILPATRICK ON THE CLYDE AND CONSISTED OF A TURF RAMPART BEHIND A WIDE AND DEEP DITCH. ALONG THE WALL LAY FORTS, FORTLETS AND BEACON-PLATFORMS, LINKED BY A ROAD. THIS IS A SECTION OF THE STONE BASE OF THE ANTONINE WALL. IT IS 4.3m (15 ROMAN ft) WIDE AND IS CROSSED BY A DRAIN. THE TURF RAMPART, PROBABLY 3-4m HIGH AND TOPPED BY A TIMBER BREASTWORK, RESTED ON THIS BASE. A ROMAN BATH-HOUSE, 1km TO THE WEST ON ROMAN ROAD, MAY BE VISITED.

Antonine Gardens

Located at the western end of the Antonine Wall several miles away, the Roman Fort just outside Glasgow was occupied between AD142 and 165.

The Bearsden Fort covered 2.4 acres, which included administrative and storage buildings, granaries, workshops, barracks and a bath complex.

The site has yielded sculpture and inscriptions, the latter showing that the fort was built by the 20th Roman Legion. The gardens were opened by Provost Joan Cameron on 28 April 1992.

The Roman Baths

The Roman bath complex was excavated between 1973 and 1979, outside local residents' front gardens.

There were many rooms excavated, including a cold bath (opposite), a cold room or frigidarium (below)…

COLD BATH

...a hot bath which had a raised floor for hot air circulation,

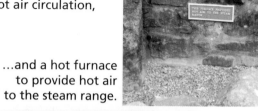

...and a hot furnace to provide hot air to the steam range.

There is a tepidarium which is the second warm room, containing a niche or a water basin.

It is also possible to see the main entrance, the changing room or Apodyterium and the path by which the soldiers used to enter.

There are modern Roman Gardens today, but not built by real Romans.

Coat of Arms

The patron saint of Glasgow was Saint Kentigern. His father was Ewan ap Urien, a prince of Strath-Clyde, and his mother was Thenaw, a daughter of Lot, King of Northumbria. Thenaw was visionary and dreamed of being a second Virgin Mary, but her paternal parent was too matter of fact, so he sent her to sea in a little boat which was ultimately driven to Culross. There Saint Kentigern was born and partly educated by Saint Serf, who latterly handed him over to the care of Semanus, Bishop of Orkney. After taking the good little boy in charge, Semanus found him so loving and kindly in disposition that he called him by a pet-name of his own – Mungo, from the Norwegian phrase Mongah (my friend or dear One) and this stuck with him, hence the name Saint Mungo. Kentigern, his first title, means Lord-in-Chief.

Glasgow's coat of arms can be found all around Glasgow. This coat of arms is located at Kelvin Bridge. This bridge crossing the River Kelvin was opened on 29 September 1891 by the Lord Provost.

Lights

There are many street lights with the Glasgow story on them. This one is located beside Glasgow Cathedral.

Glasgow has its own folklore. One particular story, taught at school, is about the bird that never flew, the tree that never grew, the bell that never rang and the fish that never swam.

The bird is a robin red breast which St Kentigren brought back to life, of which there used to be a statue on Buchanan Street.

The tree symbolises the tree which St Kentigren miraculously caused to burst into flames

The bell is a small hand bell used by saints of the Celtic Church to call their flocks to worship. It is claimed that St Mungo's bell was square in shape and given to him by the Pope.

The fish, with its golden ring, was the salmon which helped to save Queen Languoreth from the wrath of her husband, King Rydderck Hael.

The Motto of Glasgow
The full motto of Glasgow is 'Lord, let Glasgow flourish through the preaching of thy word and the praising of thy name.' By 1699 it had simply become 'Let Glasgow Flourish.' This coat of arms can be found on a tram now parked in the Glasgow Transport Museum.

Glasgow Cathedral

Glasgow Cathedral was established in AD543 and was a place for Christian worship from AD397, after it was blessed by Saint Ninian. This is the earliest missionary recorded in Scottish history. The building was completed by Robert Blacader, the first Bishop of Glasgow.

The cathedral is the only complete mediaeval cathedral still standing on the Scottish mainland. It has been called 'one of the greatest architectural treasures of the medieval period in Scotland'.

There are many grand windows and entrances to the cathedral, although the main entrance is at the side. The height of the spire is 216 feet and the building has 147 pillars.

Inside the cathedral

Inside the cathedral we can see St Mungo's Tapestry, which contains a bird, a bell, a fish and a tree – the four elements of Glasgow's coat of arms. St Mungo's tomb is located within the lower church. St Mungo died in AD603 and the ground had been consecrated for Christian burial in AD397.

The ceiling of the cathedral is a masterpiece, and it requires several miracles to clean. Looking west in the nave there are two large pillars that support the building.

There are also many beautiful stained-glass windows that come to life on sunny days.

Pictured top, this small room beside the cloisters has many smiling faces on the wall to cheer you up.

The cloisters, above, are a tranquil place to escape from the pressures of modern day life.

To the left, a large Celtic cross represents the cathedral's past in Scotland.

Opposite page: The lectern, in the form of an eagle, is located in the Quire's Chancel. It was made in France in the 18th century.

A sword located on the stairs leading from the lower church to the Blacader Aisle.

Cathedral Square Gardens

John Carrick was responsible for the design of the Cathedral Square Gardens in 1976.

One design in the garden, pictured above, simply says 'Let Peace Flourish' instead of 'Let Glasgow flourish.'

King William III

On the west side of the garden an equestrian statue of King William III can be found.

A plaque states 'In commemoration of the Tercentenary of the Glorious Rendition of 1688–1689.' In Glasgow he is known as King Billy, a Protestant king married to Queen Mary and who succeeded the Catholic King James III of Britain.

As part of Glasgow's sometimes not-so-proud history, there is a strong sectarian divide between the Protestants and the Catholics, no more so than depicted at rival team games of Rangers and Celtic.

John Knox Memorial
This 60-foot column standing at the top of the necropolis is in memory of John Knox and was designed by Thomas Hamilton in 1825. John Knox holds a Bible in his hand. He was one of Scotland's most important reformers in the 16th century.

The Royal Infirmary

To the left of the cathedral is the Royal Infirmary. The hospital has grown over the past few decades, but the statue of Queen Victoria with her orb has not changed over the years.

David Livingston

There is a statue of David Livingston outside the cathedral, sculpted by John Mossman in 1879. There are also scenes of his travels and life in Africa.

Bridge of Sighs

Built in 1833 by James Hamilton, the Glasgow Cathedral is seen from the Bridge of Sighs.

The bridge probably got its name from the sighs and cries of woe emanating from the relatives of the deceased as they made their way to the necropolis.

This memorial pictured above is for those who gave their lives in the Korean War in the 1950s.

This is Glasgow Cathedral viewed from the Zen Garden outside St Mungo's Museum.

The garden is called 'Where we are' and was designed by Yasutaro Taraka in 1993. It is an ideal place to sit and contemplate life and death, as signified by the necropolis high up on the hill.

Pictured above, a Celtic cross marks the final resting place of a wealthy merchant.

Here at the necropolis, a herd of deer has taken up residence, and can be seen early in the morning and late at night. Patients of the nearby Glasgow Royal Infirmary have many a tale to tell of their movements and habits.

To the right, a mother comforts her child on the west side of the necropolis.

39

Only the rich could afford to be buried in the large tombs of the Glasgow necropolis, built on a hill overlooking the city. No one is buried there any more.

Provand's Lordship

The Provand's Lordship, pictured above, is the oldest building in Glasgow.

Bishop Andrew Muirhead built the building in 1471 to house the chaplain of the nearby St Nicholas Hospital. The canon living here was the Lord of Provan, Provan being an area to the east of the city.

The Bishop's Castle, which stood on the east side of the Provand's Lordship, was reduced to a ruin by the middle of the 18th century and eventually demolished in 1792 to make way for the Royal Infirmary (see page 36). Part of the site, including Bishop Cameron's tower, is now occupied by the St Mungo Museum of Religious Life and Art, which opened in 1993.

Both King James II and IV visited this building during their reigns in the 15th and 16th centuries. It was completely renovated in 1996 and is one of the most frequently-visited buildings in Glasgow. The building is a Grade-A listed ancient monument, with all major repairs and conservation work subject to approval by Historic Scotland.

This room, top, belonged to Canon Cuthbert Simson, who lived in it between 1501 and 1513. He was one of the 32 canons who were responsible for the cathedral.

As we can see from the picture above, the canons in the 16th century had a lot to look forward to for dinner, mainly bread and fish.

The pietà, right, was sculpted in the 16th century and shows the Virgin Mary holding the dead body of Jesus in her lap. Pietà is Italian and means mercy or pity.

There is a cloistered garden behind Provand's Lordship, reflecting the building's possible links with the chapel and hospital of St Nicholas.

The garden, which was designed by architects James Cunning, Young and Partners, falls into two distinct parts. On the outer edge is a garden containing plants that were in common use for medical purposes in the 15th century, and at the centre is a Celtic design.

St Nicholas Gardens date from 1995, and as part of this new development, the 'Knot' Garden is based on an ancient Celtic knot design. The Glasgow coat of arms comes from the Old College in the High Street.

It is possible to walk round the garden and admire the many designs on the wall.

There is a very old sundial, pictured here on the left, high up on the outside wall.

St Andrew's
Parish Church

In and Around Glasgow Green

Glasgow Green has many statues and fountains, including the large Nelson's Monument, the beautiful Doulton Fountain and the James Martin Fountain. Around the Green are St Andrew's Parish Church, the Templeton Carpet Factory and the Glasgow Mosque.

Glasgow Green

Glasgow Green in the city centre dates as far back as 1450, when it was gifted by James II to Bishop William Turnbull to be used as a grazing ground for the burgh's animals. The present layout dates back to around 1820.

Prince Charlie inspected his troops here in the winter of 1745–46, before he was beaten by the English at Culloden. They had all received new clothes, perhaps from Princes Square.

Glasgow Green is the oldest park in Britain and was opened to the public in 1884, with 80,000 entering its gates on the first day. Glaswegians, as the friendly folk of Glasgow are called, still have the right to dry their washing here. The first steamie, or wash house, was built in 1732 at Calmachie Burn. There are many events hosted on the green, including the World Pipe Band Championship, the Great Scottish Run, annual fireworks displays and rock concerts. Glasgow Green has been called the 'lung' of Glasgow, a relationship similar to Central Park and New York.

Nelson's Monument and the People's Palace are also found on Glasgow Green.

The clothes poles on Glasgow Green are located outside the factory.

During the time of the Glasgow Green being given over to the people of Glasgow, dozens of clothes poles were built, giving local residents access to free drying on the green. A local 'steamie' was built nearby to allow the residents to wash their clothes prior to hanging them out. When it is a bright blustery day, sheets and towels can still be seen, flapping in the breeze.

There used to be a train station on Glasgow Green, but the only transport that passes by now are Glasgow Tour Buses.

The James Martin Fountain

In 1893 the James Martin Fountain was erected in his honour.

For some reason, the iron used in this fountain was not reclaimed for use during World War Two, as part of the munitions programme. It would have been a shame to destroy this beautiful memorial.

Nelson's Monument

Nelson's Monument, pictured below, was the first monument to be erected in Britain to commemorate the royal victories of Viscount Horatio Nelson (1758–1805).

David Hamilton built it in 1806, and it currently stands at 44m (144ft) tall. This was not always the case, as it was struck by lightning in 1810 – slicing six metres off the top. Nelson's famous victories are listed: Aboukir (1798), Copenhagen (1801) and Trafalgar (1805), where he was killed.

The plaque on the ground reads:

'Standing forty-four metres high, this obelisk designed by the architect David Hamilton and built by the mason A. Brockett, was the first civic monument in Britain to Nelsons victories.

The money to build the monument was raised by public subscription and the foundation stone was laid on Friday 1st August 1806.'

Nelson's Monument

James Watt

The James Watt Commemorative Stone, below, lies to the south of Nelson's monument. The inscription reads 'Near this spot in 1765, James Watt (1736–1819) conceived the idea of the separate condenser for the steam engine, patented in 1769.'

There is also a statue to his memory near the People's Palace, seen here on the left.

The Doulton Fountain

In 1888 A.E Pearce designed the Doulton Fountain, which is 14m (46ft) high.

Above, Queen Victoria features on the top of the Doulton Fountain with her orb and spectre.

In 2006 the fountain underwent extensive renovation and is working perfectly in its new location outside the People's Palace.

The Templeton Carpet Factory
William Leiper built The Templeton Carpet Factory in 1892, and it is Glasgow's most colourful brick building.

The Barras

The Barras, as seen above, Glasgow's answer to the Flea Market in Paris, is a series of indoor markets selling anything and everything. One's junk is another one's treasure.

The Barrowland Ballroom, pictured below, is a major venue for many live acts, with the Corn Exchange in Edinburgh its sister venue. After the war and well into the 70s many Glaswegians used the Barrowland Ballroom as a 'jiggin' and dancing' meeting place, where romance was in the air every Saturday night!

St Andrew's Parish Church

In remembrance of St Andrew, Scotland's patron saint, Allan Dreghorn built the St Andrew's Parish Church between 1739 and 1756.

The church is a beautiful 18th-century building which has been restored and converted into a venue that you can hire for ceildhs, concerts and weddings.

Below is a memorial outside the former St Andrew's-by-the-Green Episcopal Church. It is the oldest surviving Episcopal Church in Scotland and was built after the Jacobite rebellion of 1745.

Greenhead House

Above Greenhead House on Arcadia Street, a child can be seen reading his book. Charles Wilson built the house in 1846 as an orphanage and it is now the Greenview School.

St Andrew's Suspension Bridge

Built in 1854 by Neil Robson, St Andrew's
Suspension Bridge is considered a work
of art by the residents of Glasgow. It is
of a grand design and links the south
side with the city centre.

Dolores Ibarruis Statue

The statue, with its arms raised to the sky, is dedicated to the memory of Dolores Ibarruis, or La Passionara, who fought against Franco's army in the Spanish Civil War in the 1930s. Ibarruis died in 1989 at the age of 94. On the side of the status one inscription reads 'Better to die on your feet than live forever on your knees.'

Glasgow Central Mosque

The Coleman Ballantine Partnership built the Glasgow Central Mosque in 1984, and it was the first mosque to be built in Glasgow.

When you look at the large golden dome and the grand main entrance to the mosque, you could be anywhere in the world.

It has a tall minaret with a crescent moon, an ecumenical addition to the Glasgow skyline.

Lord Kelvin's Sundial

The University of Glasgow

The University Tower can be seen from all over Glasgow. The university contains the Cloisters, the War Memorial Chapel and many sculptures.

University of Glasgow

The main building (built in 1864–70 by Sir George Gilbert Scott) is Gothic in design and is constructed of local white sandstone. Sir Scott, the architect, was born in 1811 and died in 1878. He was knighted in 1872. He was the Professor of Architecture at the Royal Academy between 1866 and 1873, and he is now buried in Westminster Abbey.

Scott designed over 1,000 buildings in his lifetime, including the Albert Memorial (1862–63) and the Episcopal Cathedral in Edinburgh.

The university was the second largest building to be constructed in Britain since the Houses of Parliament were completed in 1860.

The main building, which was erected in stages as finances allowed, gives a feeling of grandeur as you walk around it. Every corner has its own unique architecture and embellishments.

The dates 1451 and 1870 can be seen above this entrance, pictured above, into the quadrangles. The bull represents Bishop Turnbull and the three shells represent the Marquis of Montrose, who was the chancellor in 1870.

Within the main entrance the Glasgow coat of arms, right, can be viewed with the motto of the university underneath. *Via, Veritas, Vita* translates as 'The way, the truth and the life.'

The foundation stones were laid by Alexandra, the Princess of Wales, and Edward, the Prince of Wales, in October 1863.

The University Tower

The construction of the University Tower was a father and son effort, with Sir George Scott starting the project and his son Oldrid completing it in 1887.

The dominating spire was the last part of the main building to be built. At 72 metres high it is Glasgow's most recognisable landmark and can be seen from all over the city.

Glasgow University from Partick Bridge.
The foundation stone for the bridge
was laid in 1877.

The main university building was built with two quadrangles, similar to the Old College, with the central section housing the library and the Hunterian Museum.

The entrance, left, leads from the quadrangles to the cloisters. A bench in the west quadrangle looking onto the chapel, below, is dedicated to Callum Neil Airth, who died aged 20.

This staircase originally came from the Old College on High Street, where the university was first founded. It was carried brick by brick to its present location. From its new location it was used as a link from Professors Square to the main building. When the War Memorial Chapel was built in 1929 the staircase was rotated 180 degrees to lead into Fore Hall.

A lion and a unicorn guard the staircase, their details painted in gold and sitting to attention like guards on duty. The lion represents strength and the unicorn purity. It was thought that when the two creatures fought it would result in the changing of the seasons. There is little chance of them fighting these days, as they are both covered up.

The University Cloisters

The University Cloisters were never meant to be an important feature of the university, yet it has become one of the most liked and appreciated parts of the main building.

The cloisters separate the east and west quadrangle and support the large Bute Hall and smaller Randolph Hall above it. It is possible to see the War Memorial Chapel through the arches facing west, while facing east you can see the Geography Department.

Everywhere you turn the light shines upon a part of the cloisters, sending other parts into darkness. The area is a photographer's paradise.

Pearce Lodge

Sir William Pearce (1833–88) funded the building of this lodge, and therefore it was named after him. There is a statue erected of him near his institute in Elder Park in Govan. The institute was first used by the Professor of Naval Architecture, a link to the shipbuilding tradition of Sir Pearce.

Parts of the Pearce Lodge (built in 1885–88 by Alexander Thomson) came from the original 17th-century Old College stone by stone.

The large gate has been painted gold to brighten up the building, and there is a great amount of detail as you walk through the lodge. The arches would inspire any student who uses this as a shortcut.

The turrets seem to touch the sky, and when you look up you can see the Latin Inscription *'Hae ae des extructae sunt anno dom'* and the date 1656 written in a mediaeval version of Roman numerals. You can also see Charles II's royal coat of arms and his motto *'Honi soit qui mal y pense'*, which means 'Evil to him who evil thinks.'

Just outside the lodge a statue of St Kentigren is etched in an archway.

The Reading Room

The Reading Room became the new library and is located across the other side of University Avenue from the main building. The architects, T. Harold Hughes and D.Waugh, won an award for its design in 1939. They would go on to build the chemistry building 10 years later. The building is just one large room with smaller rooms on the upper level.

A plaque outside states that 'the library was built within the grounds of Hillhead House which was presented to the university in 1917.' In the years to come, as the university expanded it would occupy many of the houses which were located around its perimeter.

A statue of St Mungo stands above the doorway.

The McIntyre Building

The McIntyre Building (built in 1886, 1893 and 1908 by Sir J.J. Burnett) houses the Student Representative Council and the rector's office, together with a John Smith Bookshop and a second-hand bookshop. It was originally built as a male-only student union.

The university's main library, above, would not be built until 1968.

The James Watt Engineering Building

A year after the completion of the chemistry building, work started on the expansion to the east of the main building, beside the Pearce Lodge, to house the engineering department. The main building proved too small by the end of the 1950s, and the 1960s marked the start of the modern expansion of the university.

A large bas relief by Eric Kennington, finished in 1957, can be viewed on the building. On closer inspection it can be seen how engineering has changed over the years.

75

The Wolfson Medical School Building

The Wolfson Medical School Building (built in 2002 by Reiach & Hall) is the newest building on campus. It was built to mark the 150th anniversary of the university at the Gilmorehill Site, and it was placed where the old nurses halls of residence used to be, which was demolished five years before.

The Anderson College

The Anderson College is named after John Anderson FRS (1726–1796), who was a professor at the university. He left the building to start a rival university, Strathclyde, which was given to Glasgow University in 1947.

Looking up above the main entrance, pictured above, you can see a carving on the wall. This was done by Pittendrigh MacGillivray and shows a patient having his pulse taken while other doctors monitor his condition.

The War Memorial Chapel

The War Memorial Chapel (built in 1923 by Sir J.J. Burnett) was erected in memory of the 733 men associated with the university who died during World War One and Two, and it was built to complete the west quadrangle and the main building.

It took five years to build and the original plans by the architects can be seen inside the chapel. During term time there is a 10-minute service starting at 8.45am.

It is an ecumenical chapel and all chaplains and ministers from every denomination take part in the morning service.

The Pontecorvo Building

The Pontecorvo Building (opposite) houses the molecular genetics department and was built in 1967, regarded by many as an eyesore. G.P.A. Pontecorvo FRS (b.1907) demonstrated mapping within genes and was a pioneer of Aspergillus genetics.

Inside the chapel and to the east there are three large windows by Lawrence Lee and St Mungo; the Patron Saint of Glasgow stands underneath.

The western end of the chapel has a large rose window that shows the virtues of civic life as well as bearing a coat of arms in the centre. There are also many decorations on the pews and lecterns.

Pictured below are names of all the students who have died in the World Wars.

The Quincentenary Gates, above, were erected by the General Council to mark the 500th anniversary of the university in 1951. Through the gates and looking south the main building and the Hunter Memorial can be seen, and looking north the Reading Room is visible. On the gate there are the names of 28 well-known people associated with the university over the 500 years. A lion and a unicorn stand on either side of the gate, seen here to the right.

The Sculptures

Sculptures around the campus include a bronze sculpture called *Diagram of an object* by Dhurva Mistry (1990). It is a modern representation of a mother with child and is located outside the Hunterian Art Gallery.

Three Squares Gyratory, pictured above, is located in the west quadrangle and is a mobile sculpture that blows about in the wind. It was designed by George Rickey in 1972.

A sculpture called *Sections Extending* (two cast in-situ), by Zeyad Dajani in 1996, is located outside the refectory.

84

Lucy Aird designed this stainless steel structure on the side of the Rankine Building. It is called *1840–1990* and celebrates the 150th anniversary of the founding of the Regius Chair of Civil Engineering and Mechanics.

Knowledge and Inspiration, by Walter Pritchard, was completed in 1960. The seated man represents knowledge and the smaller female figure represents inspiration. The sculpture is situated on the outside of the Modern Languages building.

Wellington Church

Wellington Church is located on University Avenue. It was built in 1884 and designed by Thomas Watson.

It is of very grand design, reminiscent of a large Greek Temple. It is Church of Scotland and still in use every Sunday.

The Gilmorehill Halls

The Gilmorehill Halls were built in 1876 by James Sellars. It is home to the G12 theatre, which produces new musicals and plays and also has a cinema.

It houses the Department of Theatre, Film and Television Studies. The building also has some marvellous stained-glass windows.

Glasgow University Union

Across the road from the G12 theatre is the Glasgow University Union. This was built in 1930 and designed by A. McNaughton. It was established in 1885 and many students enjoy the beer garden, even when it is not sunny.

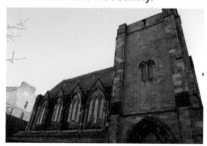

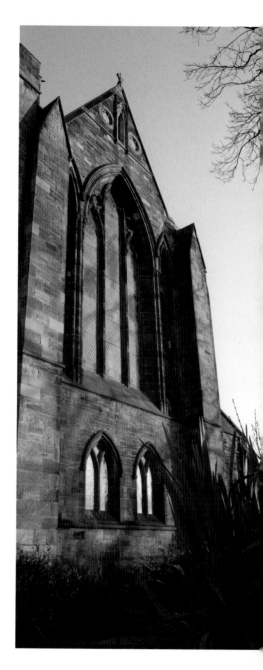

The west entrance to Kelvin Grove Park on Park Circus. The lights neither work nor are maintained.

Kelvin Way Bridge

There are four pairs of large statues decorating the four corners of the Kelvin Way Bridge designed by Paul Raphael Montford, and they were erected six years after their commissioning in 1914.

The bridge crosses the River Kelvin at the art galleries.

Commerce looks after a bag of money while Industry holds a large sledge-hammer.

Philosophy looks deep in thought while Inspiration holds a lute.

Peace sits by a spinning wheel while War screams victoriously after winning a battle.

Navigation holds a tiller in his hand while Shipbuilding holds a wooden hull in one hand and a mallet in the other.

The Highland Light Infantry Memorial

The Highland Light Infantry Memorial (built in 1906 by J. Rhind) is a memorial to all those who died in the South African Wars of 1899–1902 and shows a sentry guarding a bridge. The infantry were raised 71st in 1777 and 74th in 1787. Their museum can be found at 518 Sauchiehall Street, Glasgow. The soldier was originally armed with a large sword. However, by 2007 the sword tip had broken off.

The men who died are put into three distinct classes, 'Officers, non-commissioned officers, and men.' Private Charles Thomas Kennedy (24) was awarded the Victoria Cross for his courageous act during the South African War in 1900. On 22 November 1900 at Dewetsdorp, South Africa, he carried a wounded comrade who was bleeding to death from Gibraltar Hill to the hospital almost a mile away under heavy fire. His Victoria Cross is displayed in their museum.

The Prince Of Wales Bridge

The Prince Of Wales Bridge crosses the River Kelvin at the Highland Light Infantry Memorial.

There was a temporary bridge here in 1868 to allow the Prince of Wales to lay the foundation stone of Glasgow University.

It was designed by Alex McDonald in 1895 and is now used by students, not princes.

Field Marshall Roberts

This is a statue of Field Marshall Roberts, Lord Frederick Sleigh, Baron Roberts of Kandahar, KP, GCB, GCSI, GCIE, VC (1832–1914), who took part in the Indian Mutiny.

There is a replica of this statue in Calcutta.

The memorial reads:

TO THE GLORIOUS MEMORY OF ALL RANKS
THE CAMERONIANS (SCOTTISH RIFLES) WHO.
TO UPHOLD LIBERTY AND JUSTICE IN THE WORLD.
LAID DOWN THEIR LIVES IN THE TWO WORLD WARS
1914 – 1918 AND 1939 – 1945.

The Cameronians War Memorial

The Cameronians War Memorial (built in 1924 by P. Lindsay Clark) is dedicated 'to the glorious memory of all ranks of the Cameronians who, to uphold liberty and justice in the world, laid down their lives during the two World Wars'.

The 7th Batallion were raised 26th in 1689 and 90th in 1794. The Cameronian regiment was disbanded in 1968. Their regimental headquarters and museum is located at 129 Main Street in Hamilton. The statue shows one man 'going over the top' while two of his comrades provide him with cover. His fist is clenched as he looks forward with his head held high.

These three soldiers are willing to die so that future generations have the kind of freedom we are used to today, allowing us to visit such places as the Transport Museum and art galleries, or study at Glasgow University.

The Normandy Veterans Memorial

The Normandy Veterans Memorial was erected in 1994.
An inscription reads: 'To the eternal memory of our comrades who laid down their lives in the Battle of Normandy on 6th June to 20th August 1944.'

Charing Cross Mansions

Architecture

Charles Rennie Mackintosh is Glasgow's best-known architect. His works include the Mackintosh House, House for an Art Lover, Glasgow School of Art and the Willow Tea rooms. Alexander Thomson has also contributed his own style to Glasgow's buildings, including Moray Place and the Egyptian Halls.

Charles Rennie Mackintosh

Charles Rennie Mackintosh is Glasgow's most famous architect, who was born in 1868 and died in 1928. He and his wife originally stayed at 78 Southpark Avenue (pictured above), which is now a car park beside the refectory. The house was built in 1906 and he lived there until 1914. He was important in facilitating the trend of moving away from the city centre to the West End.

In 1978 a reconstruction of his house was built facing the same direction to allow the correct natural lighting to enter, as Mackintosh would have wanted.

The main door is located several feet above the main road, but at the original house on Southpark Avenue the door would obviously have been on street level. Luckily there is another entrance which is more accessible. The rooms are exactly as Mackintosh had designed them.

The windows on the side of the building are very characteristic of his style.

The House for an Art Lover

The House for an Art Lover was built on the foundations of the Ibrox Hill House, which was demolished in 1913. It is an excellent resource for visitors as both a contemporary conference centre and cultural attraction. The House for an Art Lover was designed by Charles Rennie Mackintosh in 1901 but was not built until a grant enabled the construction of the building between 1989 and 1996 in Bellahouston Park, on the south side of Glasgow. Visitors can compare the original Mackintosh designs against each completed room.

In his day Mackintosh was capable of not only being modern, but even before his time.

The Walled Garden, below, is to the west of the house and was used as the kitchen garden of Ibrox Hill House. There is a kaleidoscope of colours during the summer that augments the house perfectly.

Outside the main gardens is a sculpture, pictured below, for all those men who made the Clyde great.

The Willow Tea Rooms

In 1903 Charles Rennie Mackintosh converted an old warehouse in Sauchiehall Street into the Willow Tea Rooms for Mrs Kate Cranston, who owned several popular tearooms throughout the city. Willow trees once grew on Sauchiehall Street, hence the name given to the tea rooms.

Scotland Street Museum

Scotland Street Museum was also built by Charles Rennie Mackintosh, in 1905. It was a fully operational school until 1979, when it lay derelict for 11 years until it was converted into a museum in 1990.

There are many of Mackintosh's characteristic designs on show, including the windows, curved stairways and the conical roofs.

There were two entrances, one for the girls and one for boys.

There is still the original bell, pictured here on the right, on the side of the wall.

When you walk about Glasgow and look up, there are many interesting designs on the buildings.

For example, pictured above is a carving of a blindfolded woman, perhaps suggesting that justice is blind.

Not many people know about the bust of Beethoven, which is found at 341 Renfrew Street, parallel to Sauchiehall Street. This used to be a music shop and with Beethoven watching over you, you would have to feel inspired to buy a piano or violin.

Pictured here is a lion showing its teeth ready to pounce. The Lion Rampart is on the Scottish flag.

This lady with the building on her shoulders is found at the Merchant's House Building (built in 1874 by J. Burnett) at 7 West George Street. Looking up you can see the Merchant's House motto *Toties redeuntis eodem*, which means 'So often returning to the same place.'

Further down the street, a Greek male's head keeps an eye on the shoppers below.

Two men appear from inside the building as if looking out from an office window.

Charing Cross

Many red sandstone tenements were razed to the ground to make way for the motorway. Local residents made loud but futile protestations to stop the building of the M8 which was, not considered progress at the time.

Now a monstrosity of a modern building hangs over the motorway, hiding Glasgow's Victorian architecture from the passing world.

J.J. Burnett who was involved in some of the Glasgow University buildings, built the Charring Cross Mansions in 1891. It has a tall cupola with a surrounding railing.

The building displays the initials RS & S, as it was built for the warehousemen Robert Simpson and Sons. There is a baroque clock, beautifully decorated, and statues further enhance the building's appearance.

In Woodlands Road there is another building displaying the Glasgow coat of arms.

M8

W.A. Fairhurst and Partners built the Kingston Bridge in 1968, spanning 150 feet over the River Clyde. The motorway is unique in that it passes through the heart of the city, not around it. However, the bridge is closed in August due to the Great Scottish Run.

Some parts of the motorway were never finished, leaving 'roads to nowhere'.

Charing Cross Fountian

Built in 1896 in honour of Sir Charles Cameron, BART, DL and LLD in recognition of his service to Glasgow and Scotland during his 21 years in Parliament 1874–95, the Cameron Memorial Fountain can be found at Charing Cross, leaning slightly to the east. A famous Glasgow landmark, it has moved from site to site, with its final resting place at Woodside Crescent off Sauchiehall Street.

So many businesses were torn down to make way for the motorway, while the new offices lack the subtle charm of the early 20th century.

St George Street Mansions

Both Charing Cross Mansions and St George's Mansions were designed by Burnet and Boston in 1900, and they still remain.

The motorway carries thousands of cars through the city centre every hour, sometimes at the speed of light and other times at a speed similar to the early horse and cart.

St Jude's

St Jude's Free Presbyterian Church can be found on Woodlands Road. This building was also designed by John Burnet in 1875. A great selection of theology books and Bible study guides are available from the church.

The Mitchell Library

The impressive Mitchell Library is the centre of the public library system of Glasgow and is one of the largest public reference libraries in Europe.

There is a great deal of decorative architecture on all sides of the building, especially on Granville Street. Its distinctive copper dome was erected in 1911.

After 1971 Glasgow rediscovered its architecture, and buildings were repaired and grime from years of pollution was removed, including the public library.

Lobby Dosser

Also on Woodlands Road is a statue of Lobby Dosser, a character created by Bud Neil. Bud was an innovative cartoonist who worked for the Glasgow newspapers. Lobby sits on El Fideldo, his trusted two-legged horse.

Behind the library is the Mitchell Theatre where Atlas can be seen holding the world near the main entrance.

The Kelvinside Terrace Steps

Just a few minutes walk from the Botanic Gardens are the Kelvinside Terrace Steps, designed by Alexander Thomson in 1872.

Moray Place

This large terrace, designed by Alexander Thomson, is called Moray Place, and it is hidden off Pollokshaws Road. Thomson stayed in number one, which was expanded in the 1930s. All his characteristic details are present.

Great Western Terrace

Great Western Terrace was designed by Alexander Thomson in 1869. Sir William Burrell lived at number eight from 1902 to 1927.

The Hiton Hotel

The Hiton Hotel is now located on Grosvenor Terrace and it was built in 1855 and designed by John Rochead.

Kelvinside Parish Church

Located at the top of Byres Road, this pub and nightclub used to be the Kelvinside Parish Church. It was designed by J.J. Stevenson in 1862, and before it was converted into a pub it was the Glasgow Bible College.

Glasgow Streets

The main streets in Glasgow feature the 'Z' shape of Sauchiehall Street, Buchanan Street and Argyle Street, and they are home to the largest collection of major retail outlets outside London. Byres Road is located in the West End and has a large variety of pubs and restaurants in the surrounding lanes.

Buchanan Street

The street was first opened in 1780 and was named after Andrew Buchanan of Buchanan, a successful tobacco merchant.

At the bottom of the street is St Enoch Square; St Enoch, or St Thenew, was the mother of St Mungo.

St Enoch Centre

Reiach and Hall built the St Enoch Centre between 1981 and 1989, on the site of the St Enoch Hotel and the St Enoch railway station.

The old building, which is now a travel information centre, has not changed in 100 years.

The St Enoch Hotel, on the other hand, has moved to the south end of the square and is only a fraction of the size of the original.

Princes Square

Above the entrance of Princes Square and standing on the roof, a sculpture of a peacock can be seen.

Pictured below is the stunning mosaic floor on the basement level of Princes Square.

Foucalt Pendulum

Looking down from an escalator you can see the Foucalt Pendulum, named after Jean Foucalt, who, in the 18th century, showed that the Earth rotated on its axis.

The glass roof allows natural light to pour in, creating a pleasant and relaxing atmosphere far from the city life outside.

The Argyll Arcade

The Argyll Arcade was built in 1828 by John Baird I, and it is home to many jewellers' shops.

Sloan's Place

At the junction of Virginia Street and Argyle Street, parallel to Buchanan Street, there is a discreet plaque recording the fact that Robert Burns lodged at this spot in 1787 and 1788 in the Black Bull Inn, which was built in 1759.

Sloan's Restaurant is arguably the oldest restaurant in Glasgow, built in 1798 in Morrison's Court behind the now famous Princes Square.

Royal Concert Hall

In an urban picnic spot outside the main entrance to the Royal Concert Hall, many office workers are able to enjoy the sunshine. It was designed in 1990 by Sir Leslie Martin, as one of the buildings created for Glasgow's year as the European City of Culture. The Concert Hall is primarily home to the Royal Scottish National Orchestra, although it has created a special place where all genres of music can be played.

At the front entrance there is the Glasgow coat of arms, as well as a statue of Donald Dewar at the main entrance. John Lewis is the main shop featured in the Buchanan Galleries, Glasgow's main shopping attraction.

Sauchiehall Street

Sauchiehall Street was built on a meadow or a haugh, where saugh and willow trees used to grow, and it is only partially pedestrianised. A statue of Britannia holding her shield and three-pronged trident can be seen above the buses.

In 1914 John Fairweather was responsible for the Vitograph Cinema and the winged angel playing a flute above the building.

Pictured to the right is Sauchiehall Street looking east from Cambridge Street. On the immediate right the classic architecture remains, but on the middle right the vast department stores Copland and Lye and Pettigrew and Stephens made way for Sauchiehall Street Centre, not one of Glasgow's most outstanding new buildings. In fact, it has had to be revamped twice since it was built, and finally it was taken over by the Irish Group Primark.

King's Theatre
Around the corner is the King's Theatre, built in the early 1900s by Frank Matcham. On the corner is a lion holding a shield with the letters KT on it. It can hold 2,000 people and is still a popular venue today.

Argyle Street

First known as Dumbarton Road, then changed to Wester Gate, and prior to assuming the patronymic of Archibald, Duke of Argyle, Argyle Street was originally known as Anderson Walk. Pictured here is the Adelphi Hotel which became Boots corner. It is now a fast food outlet and a book shop.

The Duke of Wellington

Sculpted by Baron Carlo Marochetti in 1844, the statue of the Duke of
Wellington can be found outside the Gallery of Modern Art (GOMA). After
his famous victory at Waterloo in 1815, he became the British prime
minister between 1828 and 1830.

Gallery of Modern Art

The Gallery of Modern Art was built in 1778 as Cunninghame Mansions, home to one of Glasgow's wealthy tobacco merchants. It then became the Royal Exchange, the city's main business centre.

There are four sections in the gallery corresponding to the four elements – earth, air, fire and water.

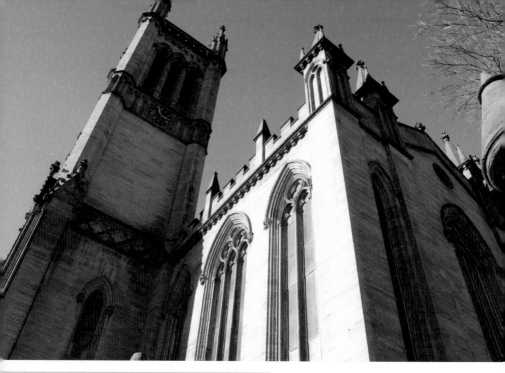

Ramshorn Kirk

Along from Queen Street on Ingram Street, in 1826, Thomas Richman erected the Ramshorn Kirk, otherwise knows at St David's Church.

A 300-year-old graveyard is located behind the kirk, right in the heart of Glasgow's city centre.

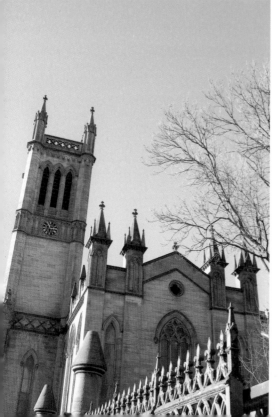

Ca'd'Oro building

The Ca'd'Oro building was originally built as a furniture warehouse.

It was designed by John Honeyman and named after a restaurant established in 1927, and its name in Venetian means 'Golden House'. It caught fire in 1987 but was later reconstructed in its original form.

The Egyptian Halls

The Egyptian Halls are further down Union Street and were designed by
Alexander Thomson.

St Stephen's Church

Renfield St Stephen's Church on Bath Street is one of the few city churches still thriving. It was the first example of 'Tractorian' Gothic design.

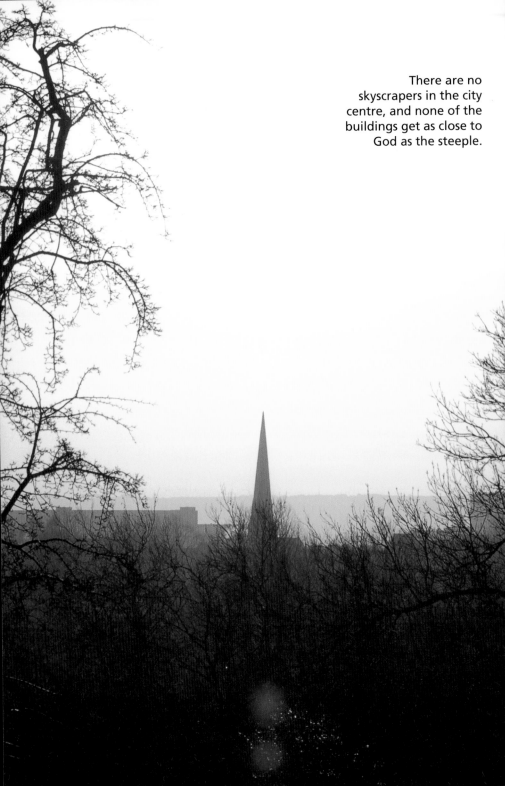

There are no skyscrapers in the city centre, and none of the buildings get as close to God as the steeple.

Dalmore House

The reflection of Dalmore House appears clearly in the windows of 301 St Vincent Street. The Miller Partnership was responsible for its design in 1990, two years after 301 St Vincent Street was built.

The building was going to be so extensive that it bent one of the major rules of town planning, namely the grid system, and it was built across the foot of Elmbank Street. This meant that traffic could not make its way down from the city centre to the Clyde at this point.

Spectrum House

Spectrum House appears as though it is wrapped in silver foil, causing it to stand out from the other buildings in Anderston.

St Vincent Street Church of the Free Church of Scotland

Alexander 'Greek' Thomson was Glasgow's next well-known architect after Charles Rennie Mackintosh. Most of his buildings were destroyed in the 1960s but there are some still standing. This is the St Vincent Street Church of the Free Church of Scotland, designed in 1859 in the Romantic Classical style.

Standing tall and proud against the anonymous office blocks which surround it, like all his work there is a Greek feel to the church, with his usual inscription clearly visible if you look up.

It is now on the World Monuments fund's list of the 100 most endangered sites.

St Columba's Gaelic Church

St Columba's Gaelic Church, built originally in 1903 by W. Tennent and F.W. Burke, is also reflected in 301 St Vincent Street offices. It has a 60m (200ft) tower, which stands tall above the surrounding tower office blocks.

Bucks Head Warehouse Building

Alexander Thomson erected the Bucks Head Warehouse Building in 1862. It was originally built for Henry Leck, a wealthy accountant.

Curlers

Curlers is the oldest pub in the West End and dates from the 17th century. It was built beside a pond used for curling, and legend has it that King Charles II granted the pub a seven-day licence.

Byres Road

Byres Road is the centre of Glasgow's West End. It runs from Dumbarton Road at Partick north to Great Western Road at the Botanic Gardens.

There is a legend on one of the buildings that reads 'Victoria Cross', which remembers the attempt to change the name from Byres Road to Victoria Road in honour of Queen Victoria.

At first glance Byres Road may seem to consist of shops, tenements and pubs, but hidden behind it is a large tennis court.

There are many gift shops on Byres Road, including Papyrus, pictured above.

Affectionately nicknamed a blue 'tardis', the blue police boxes were introduced in Great Britain in 1930 and designed by Gilbert McKenzie-Trench, with 300 in Glasgow. This one, pictured above, now sells coffee. One can still be found beside Borders Bookshop in Buchanan Street and another on Wilson Street. A total of only 12 remain in Great Britain today, with Glasgow having three of them.

Ashton Lane

There are many lanes and by-ways off Byres Road, the most popular of these is Ashton Lane.

When visiting this lane you can enjoy a coffee outside one of the many bars and restaurants. There is also a large cinema that has undergone a great transformation, which can be found in the centre of the lane.

Gardener Street

One of the steepest streets in Glasgow is Gardener Street, in Partick.

Dumbarton Road

Dumbarton Road passes through Whiteinch and Partick.

Dowanhill Park

Many locals over the years have sat on the park bench in Dowanhill Park, watching the world pass by.

George Square

George Square is located in the centre of the city. It is home to many statues including Rabbie Burns, Queen Victoria and Sir Walter Scott, with the City Chambers, home to Glasgow City Council, located on the east side of the square.

George Square Statues

Above: *Robert Peel* by John Mossman (1859). Robert Peel founded the modern police force before going on to be prime minister in 1834 and in 1841.

Top left: *Prince Albert* by Baron Carlo Morchetta in 1866. Both Prince Albert and Queen Victoria sit on horseback facing the world together, running away from the City Chambers.

Left: *Queen Victoria* by Baron Carlo Marochetta in 1854. Queen Victoria was queen from 1837 to her death in 1901. The statue was first erected in St Vincent Place before being moved here when Prince Albert's statue was unveiled.

Above: *James Watt* by Sir Francis Chantrey (1832). James Watt was an important figure in the Industrial Revolution, making steam engines a reality. His statue depicts him reading over his manuscripts.

Top right: *Sir John Moore* by John Flaxman in 1819. Sir John Moore was born in Glasgow and fought as a Lieutenant with the British Army during the War of Independence.

Right: *Sir Walter Scott's Column* by David Rhind in 1837 and the sculpture by A.H. Ritchie. The statue has Scott with his plaid over his right shoulder in the manner of the Border shepherds.

Above: A monument to *James Oswald* by Baron Carlo Marochetti in 1856. James Oswald was a very wealthy merchant who had a role in the politics of his day.

Top left: *Thomas Campbell* by John Mossman in 1877. Thomas Campbell was a poet as well as the rector of Glasgow University. He does not stand with a cigarette in his hand but a feather quill.

Left: *Thomas Graham* by William Brodie in 1871. Thomas Graham was a great chemist who became Professor of Chemistry at the Anderson College. He sits thinking over an important manuscript.

Top left: *William Gladstone* by W.H. Thornycroft in 1902. William Gladstone was prime minister in the late 1890s. He stands in his robes as he was rector of Glasgow University.

Top right: *Lord Clyde* by J.H. Foley in 1867. Lord Clyde was a field-marshal who fought all around the world, including Jamaica. He rests on a palm tree and has a telescope in his hand.

Right: *Robert Burns* by George Ewing in 1877. Robert Burns is the nation's favourite poet. He holds a daisy in his left hand in memory of his 1786 poem *To A Mountain Daisy*.

Unknown Glasgow

Garnethill is home to the Glasgow Film Theatre, the Glasgow School of Art and Garnet Park, and is located to the north of the city centre. The Italian Centre is in the heart of Glasgow and is home to the best Italian designer shops, including Armani and Versace.

Garnethill

In 1810 Thomas Garnet built an observatory at the top of one of Glasgow's seven hills, and the area built on this hill was named Garnethill.

The Glasgow School of Art

The Glasgow School of Art is located inside Garnethill. It was designed by Charles Rennie Mackintosh, and so there is no reason for the students who attend not to pass with flying colours.

St Aloysius' Roman Catholic Church

In 1910 Charles Menart built St Aloysius' Roman Catholic Church. Above the door the Latin inscription reads '*Divo Aloysio Sacrum*', which translates as 'dedicated to St Aloysius'.

Garnethill Park

Another famous cityscape, opened in 1991 in the Garnethill area, was the Garnethill Park, with a small brook cascading over stones from a previously demolished tenement building.

Within the park there is also a large mural of 200,000 pieces of tile, which was created in 1978 and is located on the east side of the park.

The Glasgow Film Theatre

In 1938 W.J. Anderson built the Glasgow Film Theatre, or, to give it its original name, the Cosmopolitan, which would show alternative films then and continues to do so now.

Garnethill School

Pictured on the right is the Garnethill School, which was built in 1878 and designed by James Thomson.

Garnethill View

The view of Garnethill, over the West End from Hill Street, is both beautiful and unexpected.

The Italian Centre

In an area of Glasgow, known as the Merchant City, the Italian Centre has been so named because of the Italian fashion houses it boasts, particularly Versace and Armani. It is even possible to enjoy a coffee outside on the sidewalk, as is so common in Italy. Looking up, there are statues of Italia decorating the Italian Centre.

Shona Kinloch designed this piece of city art, a sculpture called *Thinking of Bella,* with a man and a dog staring into the night sky. The centre was designed by Page and Park architects, who often use art in their architecture.

This cleverly-designed cityscape, a waterfall, can be found in the Italian Centre square.

Glasgow Museums

The Kelvingrove Art Galleries and Museum has recently been refurbished and is Glasgow's must-see museum. Other museums in Glasgow include the People's Palace, featuring arguably one of the best comedians in the world, Billy Connolly, St Mungo's museum of religious life and art and the Burrell Collection.

The Burrell Collection

William Burrell collected thousands of pieces of art and antiquities, subsequently donating his collection to the city of Glasgow.

Today the Burrell Collection is located within the Pollok estate on the south side of Glasgow. The building was opened in 1983 and includes sections about ancient civilisations, Oriental art, stained-glass windows and near Eastern carpets and ceramics.

Presented to Glasgow in 1944 by the millionaire ship owner Sir William Burrell, the collection was amassed over the 80 years of his life and is outstanding in its diversity. Only half of the 8,000 items are displayed at any one time in the specially constructed building.

Some of the exhibits are even built into the fabric of the gallery, helping to display ancient stonework and stained-glass windows at their best.

A restaurant and café offer welcome refreshments to visitors.

Among the many pieces of art on display is Auguste Rodin's famous sculpture *The Thinker*, which he created in 1880. One of Burrell's fountains can be found close to the front entrance, and a woodpecker carving can be seen on the road leading out of Pollok Country Park.

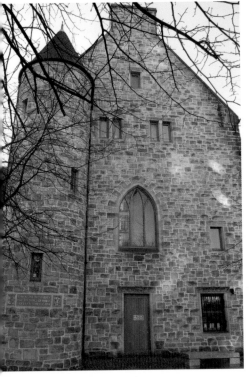

St Mungo's Museum of Religious Life and Art

Opened in 1993 and built by Ian Begg, St Mungo's Museum of Religious Life and Art is named after Glasgow's patron saint and was the first museum in the world to be dedicated solely to the study of religion. Its three main halls depict Art, World Religions and Religion in Scottish History.

Yasutaro Tanaka designed the museum's Zen Garden in 1993. Full of Buddhist symbolism, it is the only Zen Garden in Scotland and is titled 'Where we are'.

For a perfect view of the garden it is best to go to the second level of the St Mungo's Museum.

People's Palace

The museum is still the 'people's' museum and shows the way of life in the tenements of Glasgow before, during and after World War Two, at the cinema, the dance halls, the theatre and the queen's coronation. It was opened in 1898 by Lord Rosebury.

The People's Palace tells the story of Glasgow from 1175 to the present day and shows the growth of trade and industry, women's suffrage, entertainment and sport, housing and the two World Wars.

The exterior of the Winter Gardens of the People's Palace looks as though it has not changed much over the years, but there is a story behind this. It had been allowed to run into disrepair, but after several years of deciding whether it could or would survive, money was raised for it to be completely overhauled.

Some of the exhibits on display inside the People's Palace.

They include *The Steamie* (below), a dairy shop (bottom right), and an air raid shelter used during the wars (top right).

The Kelvingrove Art Gallery

The Kelvingrove Art Gallery was completed in 1901 and was built by J.W. Simpson and E.J. Milner Allen.

It is a marvellous building with many dramatic turrets and spires. The main entrance faces the River Kelvin, as the art gallery was the centrepiece of the 1901 exhibition and other buildings were built facing this entrance. It has been said that the building was built back to front, but the architect did not want the main entrance to face the busy Dumbarton Road, instead he wanted it to look over the beautiful River Kelvin.

No matter what the season, the art gallery is one of the most beautiful buildings in Glasgow. The outside hasn't changed much over the past 100 years, and it has recently undergone a multi-million pound makeover, increasing its value to the people of Glasgow.

Lord Kelvin and Lord Lister sit across the river from the Art Gallery.

Pictured below is *The Threshold* by Mary Buchanan, from around 1923. Mary was from Glasgow and won an Honourable Mention at the Paris Salon exhibition of 1923.

Below is *Paul and Virginia* by William Marshall, made from plaster in 1841. Paul is shown bravely carrying his devoted playmate over a raging river, perhaps the River Kelvin. She later dies at sea and Paul dies of a broken heart.

The Museum of Transport

The Museum of Transport is located on the River Kelvin behind the Kelvin Hall Sports Arena. The museum has trams and vintage vehicles, as well as an old-fashioned street called Kelvin Street.

Residential Glasgow

This chapter looks at houses and shops in the various other parts of Glasgow, including Firhill, Govan, Drumchapel and Ibrox.

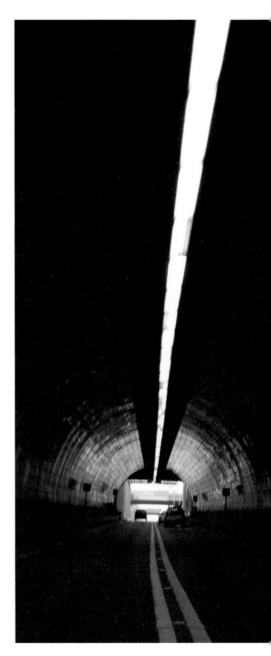

The Clyde Tunnel

The Clyde Tunnel carries thousands of cars underneath the River Clyde every hour. It takes vehicles from Jordanhill in the north, to Govan in the south.

Queen Elizabeth opened the first tunnel on 3 July 1963. Only a few years after the tunnel was completed, the Erskine Bridge was built further down the Clyde.

It is tradition to try to hold your breath while in the tunnel, but not during rush hour. The average journey time at 30mph is just under one minute.

Southbrae Drive

Southbrae Drive is one of the longest streets in Jordanhill, joining Crow Road and Anniesland Road.

Houses on the left-hand side of the street can have a free view of track and field events at the Scotstoun Leisure Centre, which opened in 1994.

Jordanhill

Some houses have the luxury of their own driveways, but for many houses in Jordanhill parking can be a lottery.

There was talk of a new railway station for the students at Strathclyde University, but for the time being they still have to walk from Jordanhill to the university.

Anniesland

Anniesland is a very busy district that is located on Great Western Road, several miles from the West End and only 50 miles from Loch Lomond.

There is one lonely high-rise flat looking over Anniesland, which is lit up on both sides. Built in 1968 it is 22-storeys high, and it is now a listed building.

It has been suggested that the area took its name from a local inn at the time called Sheep Annies, which sheep drovers stopped at for a welcome refreshment.

The railway bridge (below left) crosses over the very busy road. The Anniesland Mansions was built in 1913 by H. Campbell. It has a very unusual domed corner and has the inscription 'Anniesland Mansions 1910, MH' written on the corner.

Thornwood

Thornwood is located between Broomhill and the River Clyde. Many businesses in the area have shut down but the Thornwood pub remains as busy as ever.

Knightswood

There are many shops in Knightswood, some have gone out of business, some have changed their merchandise and some have just had a new coat of paint over the years.

The old newsagent has been demolished and a new fish and chip takeaway opened up in its place. It is very doubtful that they sell fish caught in the Nolly, or the Forth and Clyde Canal, which are situated behind them.

Knightswood is the largest district in Glasgow, containing four areas. It was constructed during the late 1920s on garden suburb plans.

As well as many shops for the residents Knightswood also has a swimming pool, library, primary and secondary schools, a dance school and a nine-hole golf course affectionally called 'Royal' Knightswood.

All the streets in Knightswood are named after people and places from Ivanhoe.

The Forth and Clyde Canal has been cleaned and made more accessible to the tourists who wish to sail along her.

Broomhill

Broomhill consists mainly of tenements, which are separate residences within a house or block of flats found especially in Scotland and the US.

There are many trees lining the streets and those around Clarence Drive have many conical turrets, which were designed by John McKellar.

There are also shops and cafés along Clarence Drive as well as the Hyndland Secondary School and large playing fields on the right-hand side as you walk towards Byres Road.

Canniesburn Toll

Canniesburn Toll is found on the road to Bearsden from the city centre and there are 10,000 or so commuters who travel into the city centre along this road every day.

There are no buildings in the middle of the toll, as there have been in the past.

Kelvindale

At the bottom of Cleveden Road a new railway station was recently opened in September 2005, called Kelvindale. It is located on the Maryhill Line and runs into the city centre. The bridge crosses over the Forth and Clyde Canal.

Within Kelvindale there are many grand and moderate houses stood side by side and across the road from each other.

North Woodside Road

North Woodside Road has changed greatly over the past 100 years. Many of the traditional buildings have been replaced with houses, although one school remains in the same location.

To cheer up some of the sandstone tenements, a large phoenix has been drawn on the side of the building, pictured below.

Belmont Street

Belmont Street starts just before the Glasgow Bridge at Kelvinbridge Underground.

It is home to the Kelvin Stevenson Memorial Church, built in 1898 by J.J. Stevenson. It has a large crown structure on the top.

Park Circus

Park Circus is Italian Renaissance in style and was designed by Charles Wilson between 1857 and 1858.

Number 22 is used as a marriage suite and was built in 1874. The owner was very wealthy and no expense was spared. The inside is a heaven for wedding photographers.

Firhill

Many Partick Thistle supporters stop in for a Jaconelli's ice cream on their way to watch their team play at Firhill. The club was formed in Partick in 1876 and came to Firhill in 1909.

They are not as successful as Rangers or Celtic, but their supporters make up for it with their voices.

Jaconelli's

Jaconelli's sells some of the best ice cream in all of Glasgow.

Maryhill

Maryhill hasn't changed much over the years, although instead of tram lanes there are now bus lanes. It is named after a Mary Hill who was the owner of the Gairbraid Estate in the late 18th century.

In the middle of the pubs, betting shops and the job centre is the very popular Maryhill library.

Behind Maryhill is the Wyndford estate, also known as the Barracks. The Barracks were established in 1876 and once housed just under 1000 soldiers.

These tall flats do not fit in well with the tenement design of the West End, located only a few miles to the east. The high rise flats were practical but lack that human touch.

The Orange Hall Lodge, pictured above, is located on Sandbank Street. The road later passes underneath the viaduct leading to Cadder from Lochburn Road, which was built in 1881. There is a very popular cycle route passing over the road that terminates at Kirkintilloch.

Maryhill Locks

There are five Maryhill Locks designed by Robert Whitworth between 1787 and 1790.

These are locks 21–25, which raise the canal's basin by around 15 metres.

The canal crosses the Maryhill Road Aqueduct, which was built in 1881, just after the First and Last pub on Maryhill Road.

Drumchapel

Drumchapel was an estate built outside Glasgow's West End. It has recently undergone a massive regeneration.

The new houses are surrounded by the blue bell woods and is once again expanding and improving at a great rate.

One of the main landmarks of Drumchapel is this large water tower pictured above, which can be seen from miles away.

High above Drumchapel is the 'Witches Circle', where witchcraft is alleged to have taken place.

Ibrox

Copland Road runs through Ibrox, almost parallel to Paisley Road West.

There is a mixture of tenements and work yards, allowing the workforce to be near their workplace.

There is one question you will always be asked in Glasgow, which is what football team you support, Rangers or Celtic. If you are unsure, answer Partick Thistle.

There is a statue of John Grieg MBE that was unveiled by the chairman of Rangers, David Murray, on 2 January 2001. It is to commemorate all those who lost their lives in tragic events at Ibrox Stadium.

There are two lists of people who have lost their lives at Ibrox dating as far back as 1902, with many lives being lost on the 2 January 1971.

Across the road from the stadium is a statue of James Wilson, who was a great medical practitioner in Govan.

The Langside Battlefield Monument

The Langside Battlefield Monument, erected in 1887, is just under 20 metres high.

The Battle of Langside was fought here on 13 May 1568 between the army of Mary Queen of Scots and the Regent Moray, and the monument marks where the queen was finally defeated. The tall pillar is beautifully decorated with eagles facing out from all four corners.

Langside Hill Church was built at the end of the 19th century in 1896 by Alexander Skirving in a design that Alexander Thomson himself would be proud of. It is now a pub and restaurant.

The Victoria Infirmary

The Victoria Infirmary is one of only a few hospitals on the south side. The large building has many turrets and balconies and was built in 1890 by Campbell Douglas and Sellars.

There is an Italian restaurant outside the hospital, which has been open for more than 100 years and was originally a tea room.

Govan

Govan Old Parish Church dates from 1888 and was designed by Robert Anderson.

It is suggested that the site dates from the first millennium, perhaps as early as the sixth century.

A statue of Sir William Pearce, left, dating from 1894 stands opposite his institute. The Pearce Lodge in Glasgow University is named after him.

The Pearce Institute itself was built in 1906 and also designed by Robert Anderson. A ship can be seen high on the top of the institute.

The Aitken Memorial Fountain was erected in 1884 by the inhabitants of Govan in affectionate remembrance of John Aitken MD, who was the burgh's first medical officer of health.

Some locals in Govan have dressed the side of these tenements with startling paintings that can be seen when entering the north-bound Clyde Tunnel. One depicts a busy New York street while this one, below, lists all that Govan has to offer. It mentions Elder Library and Elder Park.

Glasgow's Parks

The Botanic Gardens holds the Kibble Palace, which has recently been refurbished. It houses many beautiful plants and sculptures. The Kelvingrove Park is located several minutes walk away. Victoria Park, with the Fossil Grove and Bingham's Pond, is located in the West End, while Maxwell Park, Elder Park and Pollok Country Park are found on the south side of Glasgow.

Kibble Palace – the Botanic Gardens

Originally the Kibble Palace was built at the Coulport home of John Kibble in 1865, but it was re-erected in the Botanic Gardens on Great Western Road at the cost of £58,321. The building houses the national collection of tree ferns.

During the summer it is a good place to enjoy the sun and an ice cream.

The Botanic Gardens used to be on the north side of Dumbarton Road, west of Claremont Street, which is now built over.

Covering an area of 2137sq m, the Kibble Palace is one of the largest glasshouses in Britain and contains a marvellous collection of tree ferns from Australia and New Zealand, as well as plants from Africa, the Americas and the Far East.

The palace has been completely restored. It was dismantled pane by pane, cleaned and then put back together in exactly the same way.

When the sun shines through the cleaned glass, it takes your breath away.

The large goldfish pond inside the palace is very popular with the children. There are various types of goldfish as well as some catfish. Luckily, today there is a fence around the pond to stop the children from falling in.

The roof contains some amazing concentric circles. The pillars are Victorian in design with all the intricate details you would expect to find. There are many beautiful statues within the palace.

Cain, by Roscoe Mullins   *Ruth*, by Giovanni Ciniselli   *Eve*, by Scipio Todalini

The Rose garden

The Botanic Gardens also has a world rose garden that was created in 2003. The Dog Rose and Scots Brier are the most well known of the native species.

Between the two greenhouses is this fountain, right, in memory of Peter Walker, which was erected in 1906.

There are many statues and memorials beside Glasgow University in Kelvin Grove Park.

Kelvingrove Park

The Stewart Memorial Fountain, designed by John Sellars in 1871, was built in memory of Robert Stewart, who was the Lord Provost with an ambitious plan to bring fresh drinking water to Glasgow from Loch Katrine some 40 miles away.

The fountain has a statue of the Lady of the Lake on top, the subject of the poem by Sir Walter Scott.

In 1868 August-Nicolas Cain created the Kennedy Monument, depicting a Royal Bengal tigress taking a dead peacock to her young cubs, of which Central Park in New York has a replica.

Locals have dubbed this statue 'The Statue of Death.'

The Psalmist

Glasgow's most eminent sculptor Benno Schotz was a shipyard worker on the Clyde before discovering his true talent.

The Psalmist is one of his most famous sculptures. It can be found on the banks of the River Kelvin very near the Art Galleries.

Some locals decided that Benno hadn't finished the job properly and have drawn a smiling face on the sculpture.

Maxwell Park

The ground for Maxwell Park was gifted by Sir John Stirling Maxwell of Nether Pollok in 1888.

Pictured here are some examples of the beautiful flowerbeds that can be found within the grounds of Maxwell Park.

The park was formally opened, together with Pollokshields Burgh Hall, in 1890.

Bingham's Pond

Three generations of Binghams ran the pond as the Glasgow Skating and Curling Club (when the weather permitted), and latterly the clubhouse was turned into a tearoom. In 1961 a third of the pond was filled in to make way for the Jury's Pond Hotel, which is still thriving today. The pond is now a bird sanctuary.

Victoria Park

For many years Victoria Park has provided a great day out for all the family.

It is a marvellous find for those who want to take time out from Glasgow life and enjoy the sunrise and feed the swans.

There are many buildings and statues to discover in the park, including the Fossil Grove, and there is also a memorial to the SS *Daphne*. A similar memorial can be found in Elder Park in Govan.

There is a plethora of swings and slides for children to use in the park.

If you get tired walking around all the paths, you can always enjoy a rest on one of the park's benches.

The statue is a memorial to those men who died during the two World Wars. The inscription reads:

'Our Beloved Dead.
To the glory of God and in grateful and everlasting remembrance of the men of Partick and Whiteinch who fell during the Great Wars.
We will remember them.'

Queen's Park

Queen's Park has entertained countless families since its creation in 1860. Sir Joseph Paxton designed it and it was considered to be one of the finest parks at the time.

The park has a large boating pond, which is more of a home to model boats than life-size ones.

There are also many paths and benches to enjoy in the park.

Elder Park

Elder Park in Govan is named after John Elder, an important founder of the Govan shipbuilding yards. The statue of John Elder has since been redecorated with an attractive yellow beard in 2007.

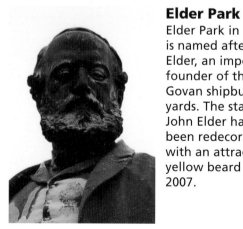

The Elder Library, above, is located just outside the park and was designed by J.J. Burnett in 1901.

The original by-laws for the park regulating its use forbade '...anyone to expose wounds or deformities inducing giving of alms...', insuring the park would remain peaceful for all.

Among all the empty beer cans and cigarette packets, this small Stonehenge can be found. It also makes a convenient resting place for the locals.

Harland and Wolff Shed, Gorvan

On the side of the Harland and Wolff Shed there is a large mural depicting the steel welders working in their yard.

Elder Park was designed by John Honeyman in 1883 and is full of ornamental stone pillars. This is the SS *Daphne* memorial made by John McArthur in 1977.

A plaque states that there was a disaster on the Clyde on the 3 July 1883 where a 500-tonne ship capsized after its launch, killing 124 workers. Today it is hard to see as it is hidden underneath some bushes.

The Govan Milestone

The Govan Milestone, by Helen Denely, was completed in 1994. It was commissioned by the Govan Housing Association. Two copper arches are balanced on top of the other, crowned by four black cormorants placed symmetrically on the curves.

Govan's Shipyards

Govan is one of Glasgow's oldest districts and dates from the sixth century. Shipbuilding and engineering transformed Govan, yet now only a few yards remain open. Beside the shipyards were the great engineering works, where generations of skilled men built the boilers for the liners, warships and other steam vessels made in Govan.

Pollok House

Pollok House is a four-storey mansion built for Sir John Maxwell, who owned the Pollok estate in 1747. It has a library, drawing room, dining room, cedar room and billiard room.

It is now owned by the National Trust, who charge an admission to enter the house. However, it is free to walk around the grounds.

There are many gardens around the house. Even the archways have been created in great detail, showing the wealth of the occupant.

The row of lime trees in the grounds is called 'Lime Avenue', and is was planted when Sir John Maxwell came of age.

The gardens around Pollok House are maintained to the highest standards. There is a small maze in the West Gardens.

Within the actual gardens there are many decorations, like the stone vase pictured at the bottom far right. They are perched on the wall around the gardens. The smiling children's faces echo the laughs of the children who have played in the gardens over the decades.

Two lions guard the entrance to the house from the river.
Outside there are highland cattle. They would not make good guard dogs but they do add to the charm of the country estate.

The War Memorial beside the White Cart Water Bridge lists 'the men from the tenantry and staff from Nether Pollok who served in the Great War (1914–1919)' in alphabetical order.

White Cart Water

The house has great views of the White Cart Water, an ideal place to have picnics by and to sail along.

The bridge over the White Cart Water dates from around 1757–58, and these dates are engraved on the side of the bridge.

In 1885 the force of the White Cart Water powered the sawmill that provided a renewable and plentiful power source for the area.

The force is still as strong today, but this power is no longer harnessed for anything.

While walking along the river some rather unusual items catch your eye. There is a carving of a Highland cow, an ancient warrior and an old plough.

Glasgow's Water

The River Kelvin is Glasgow's second-largest river and runs through the West End. The largest, the River Clyde, was once home to great shipyards and the Clydeport Crane is now its most famous landmark. Huge housing developments are being built on the site of these famous yards, the modern way of living requiring to be close to water. The Forth and Clyde Canal runs from the city centre, through the West End near the River Kelvin and out towards Bearsden in the North.

The River Kelvin

The River Kelvin is often called the 'wooded river', due to the large trees gracing its banks. The river rises in the Kilsyth Hills to the north-east of the city. Over the past 100 years many trees have flourished and grown almost as high as the tower itself.

It has been known to flood and even carry away bridges across the river, for example the Ha'penny bridge. It stood proud for 100 years until it was washed away during heavy floods on the 10 December 1994. There are many bridges still standing, however, that cross the Kelvin. The river has steep sides so the bridges are high above the water, much higher than the bridges over the Clyde.

A lot of money has been spent doing up the bridges over the years. As it nears Torrance, the river has no fancy bridges, lights or stories to tell. No boats sail along the river anymore but it serves as a reminder of all the generations who have stood and watched the river flow by them. The city has changed but the river has not.

The Clydeport Crane

The River Clyde is the 10th longest river in the UK and the third longest in Scotland. The word Clyde takes its name from the Gaelic word clith, which means 'strong'. Many great ships were built on the Clyde, and it was possible to pass under the Clyde via the two rotundas. Cowans, Sheldon and Company Limited built the Clydeport Crane, pictured here, in 1931 on Stobcross Quay.

The River Clyde, from its source in the Lowther Hills to Greenock, travels approximately 100 miles and drops 2,000ft.

The Clydeport Crane can be seen all around Glasgow and is now a List B monument, and it will never be removed from the banks of the Clyde as it is a constant reminder of the shipyards.

It is just under 60 metres tall and can lift around 200 tonnes, and there are now plans to turn it into a restaurant.

The Rotundas

Between 1890 and 1896 Wilson and Simpson built the north and south rotundas as entrances to the Harbour Tunnel. The north rotunda has six former entrances framed by tall cast-iron Corinthian columns. The tunnels were closed in 1986, but they are still standing to this day.

The north rotunda is now a successful casino and restaurant, the south rotunda is still waiting for a developer. Many tales are told about the numbers of workers crossing from one side of the Clyde to the other, but several outstanding memories include the constant dripping of water leaking from the Clyde, the single light bulbs on long flexes, the noise of boots on wooden planks and the dark creepy atmosphere, like nowhere else in this big city. It was a sad day when the tunnels closed, with families taken to the entrances to remember a romantic but dangerous past.

The PS *Waverley*

The PS *Waverley* was built in 1947 at the A & J Inglis shipyard at Pointhouse, named after the *Waverley* novels of Sir Walter Scott. She is 73m (24ft) long and 18m (58ft) wide. The engines drive two paddles, taking the ship to her cruising speed of 34mph.

The *Waverley* is very near the tall ship at Finnieston. There used to be many ships and boats like this on the Clyde, but now to spot other ships is rare.

The tall ship is called the SV *Glenlee* and is the only Clyde-built sailing ship still afloat in the UK.

The Science Centre

The Science Centre was built in 2001
and is one of Scotland's must-see
attractions.

The IMAX

The Glasgow Eye and IMAX Theatre are right beside the Science Centre. The IMAX Theatre has a large cinema screen showing films such as the *Everest Experience* and *Swimming with Dolphins*.

The Glasgow Eye

The IMAX is right next to the Glasgow Eye. The Glasgow Eye is actually a large weather vane pointing in the direction that the wind blows.

It has recently been opened to the public after being considered unsafe for several years and is now a well-known landmark around Glasgow, almost as famous as the Glasgow University Tower.

The Clyde Auditorium

Sir Norman Foster built the Clyde Auditorium on the banks of the Clyde in 1997. It seats 3,000 people, with no room for standing. There are several live bands that do not like the atmosphere of a seated crowd.

It has been affectionately nicknamed the Armadillo because of its shape and sheets of silver cladding.

The Granary

The Granary used to be the biggest brick building in Europe, but it has since been replaced by new houses. There were four brick buildings in total, comprising of over five million bricks, and it took several months to demolish it completely.

The nearby river has seen better days, too. The area is now called the Glasgow Harbour as part of an urban regeneration scheme. There are many new housing developments and on the other side of the river there is a new media village that houses the BBC and STV.

The Bell's Pedestrian Bridge

This is the Bell's Pedestrian Bridge, which crosses the Clyde at the SECC.

The new BBC building can be seen in the background.

The Glasgow Bridge

The Glasgow Bridge was completed in 1899.

There are seven arches to the bridge spanning the River Clyde.

The 'Squinty'

There has been a new bridge built across the river affectionately named the 'Squinty' bridge for obvious reasons. The bridge would be more at home in Sydney, Australia, rather than in Glasgow.

Within a few minutes walk from each other both old and new Glasgow can be seen on the river Clyde from these bridges, the river still providing much of the city's revenue.

The Broomielaw

There are still pieces of machinery left over from the bustling days when boats would come and go on the Clyde.

The first quay, with a weighhouse and cranes, was erected here in 1662. There are now luxury flats built along the river, which have nothing in common at all with the river's history.

The Forth and Clyde Canal

The Forth and Clyde Canal was built to link the east coast with the west coast, allowing passage across Scotland.

Of the five Scottish canals Glasgow had links with three: the Forth and Clyde Canal, the Monkland Canal and the Glasgow, Paisley, Johnstone and Ardrossan Canal. The network has undergone major changes and it is still possible to travel from coast to coast. The network has been developed not for industrial use, but for tourism only.

The Temple Gas Works

The Temple Gas Works were established in 1871 for the Partick, Hillhead and Maryhill Gas Company.

The two giant gas holders were built in 1893 and 1900, and they hold five million cubic feet and four million cubic feet respectively, nine million in total. No amount of painting the holders blue disguises their use, nor allows them to merge into the local landscape.

Ruchill Parish Church

Ruchill Parish Church was completed in 1905 and the church halls were designed by Charles Rennie Mackintosh before the church's building began in 1900.

Spiers Wharf

Spiers Wharf is located at the end of the Forth and Clyde Canal in the city centre. There are old buildings including the Wheatsheaf Mills, the Port Dundas Sugar Refinery and the Canal Offices, all of which date from throughout the 19th century.

Ruchill Hospital

Alex B. McDonald designed the red sandstone water tower of Ruchill Hospital. The original use of this hospital was to monitor and control infectious diseases. Now it remains closed but its grand tower and dome is still a prominent landmark, which can be seen from the canal.

Spiers Wharf